Formula

poems by

Reuben Ellis

Finishing Line Press
Georgetown, Kentucky

Formula

ACKNOWLEDGMENTS

Grateful acknowledgment is made to these journals:

"Breathing Turquoise" was previously published in *Poetry Life and Times*.
"Breathing Turquoise," "Formula," and "Causing Something to Eat" were
selected for quarter-finalist recognition by the *Nimrod International Journal*'s
2018 Pablo Neruda Prize for Poetry.
"Tearblanket," "Urine for the Spring" (new version), and "You Can Eliminate
Orange Traffic Cones" were previously published in *Adelaide Literary
Magazine*.
"Urine for the Spring" (in an earlier version) was previously published in
New Infinity Review

Publisher: Leah Maines
Editor: Christen Kincaid
Cover Art: Chris Strother
Author Photo: Robert Brian Welkie
Cover Design: Leah Huete

Printed in the USA on acid-free paper.
Order online: www.finishinglinepress.com
            also available on amazon.com

Author inquiries and mail orders:
Finishing Line Press
P. O. Box 1626
Georgetown, Kentucky 40324
U. S. A.

Table of Contents

for Rebecca

Compendium

But here you take the soil itself, tinged red and
fine grained, and eat it, take it on the skin of
your fingers, your palms, slightly wet from the
heat, and mark your forehead, your thyroid, the
denim crotch of your jeans, wherever you need
it most, your heart, because it's dying or it is
softening and large. Your body becomes a cubism
of sand, and you bring it home in the plastic
bag that held your sandwich, your pocket, your
hat, anything that can manage a cup at least, a
few ounces, or maybe a little more. You are the
protagonist in this pilot, and sand hangs from you,
like pollen. You contain. You could be
weighed and the difference would tell. The
sockets of your teeth, your entire mouth available
for speech, a kenning always ready to bust out
to make something happen. They wrap a long
scroll of butcher paper around you that trails to
the floor, drawn, stretched, spun, fibers from the
stone trees once solid with phloem. You walk
in the door leaving tracks of sand on the carpet,
but buoyant, sandy mammal how you displace,
and this is the strategy of lists, the tactic of names,
the shouting you will do any minute now, but
remember, you only have twenty-two of them.
The other six have been forgotten altogether.

Formula

Begin with the bear song,
Ya'na Ti'kanagi'ta, so
that when you sing it and
look across the small
meadow to the eucalyptus,
you will see each other
close and recall in some
dim way how you both
have changed shapes. But
now more than ever you
sing about the bear's
conception, not just its
changes or its death, in
the deep side canyons,
the narrow bottom lands
by the crest highway, and
in all the other places where
bears fuck closer by, so
that the rich smell of its
making will be heavy in
your nostrils like your
own sheets. Why are you
on your hands in the meadow?
Don't you remember what
happened last night, or
the things you said? Yes,
if you just want to see
the bear, and not kill it,
you leave certain parts of
the song out.

Causing Something to Eat

More frequently now, the fires of the chaparral
burn upward from the city, this mountainside
fictitious, a broad flue of air alone rising, and

something has caused the skin of the harsh
vertical incline, something eats it away, the
woody shrubs, the hard, leather-living leaves,

chamisa, manzanita, *Ceanothus, Cercocarpus,*
the Candles of the Lord. The boundary of the
city shifts upward, its frontier of low fire, a

spark, the unmuffled engine, the child wadding
paper towels into kindling, fireworks brought
from Indiana in a checked bag, his joint, this

smoldering condom, the untended campfire of
these penitentes, those women in the truck.
You can try saying the names of the living

things, but you must blow fluid on the child
for three nights, first on the back of the head,
then the left shoulder, then the right shoulder,

then the face. You must do this, and it must
be done indoors, so no shadow interferes, no
smoke. The child carries the weight of water.

To Destroy Shapelessness

The assertion of ugly is an assertion of complete subjectivity.
—Wendy Gilmartin

The Cartesian pints and limbs of the building probe the dune sky. The bag and dog of the building blot hardly from the grade. The dead vegetables of the building make a mold of metal, a fissure, a finial.

Because there is danger in the ugly, because its clumsiness disfigures you, its regular blemish ornaments me. The dimensional lines of its plan are ordinal chimes, movements of a disposable history of place.

To kill a building, you must find its voids, its enclosed spaces. Its blot and mar have no defense against its interior openness, this consuming gargoyle, this maw. Bring me prevalent sands, granites that can withstand.

The structure is contaminated with the urine of the architect, walking the unfinished building in the night, after the launch party with the client. Unzipping his black jeans, he holds the flashlight in his bared teeth and guides his cock with both hands as he pisses against the pedestal of his design, looking up the light beam to the abacus and frieze as he shudders with release. And it is this disposability that makes the building vulnerable, and it will dwindle, the stream atomizing so the moistness gives power to the enclosed spaces.

Mix this still air with poisonous plants, with seven earthworms beaten into paste, its sting the intercolumniation of the ceremony. Paint the doorjamb of the lobby with the mixture. That should do it.

To Treat the Methicillin-Resistant Ones

And infection follows down-wind from us,
down-touch, across the crisp surfaces against
which we abrade. Where the injured dancer
stands lithe with the antic on the steps from
the stage's wing to the arcade. His hand
caresses the tightness of her waist. Her knees
are torn, and thin creases of blood pleat the
worn fabric of her legs. After her fall to the
unforgiving deck of stage, the buffoon
comforts her. When infecting through the
broken skin, the *Staphylococcus aureus*, to
be known here from now only as the *organism*,
induces swelling, blushed redness, the bloated
rose tight with fluids, when through a wound,
surgical or accidental. The girl's pulse still
roused and vehicular from the fall, her chest
still curt and rising. And to kill the organism
before it can become loose in the blood,
please consult the oldest books first, say
Bald's Leechbook, laeceboc, its charms, its
advice and potions, hand-written, persuasively
Roman and Arabic, Yorkish, come into your
hands from trade routes and internet searches,
the exchange of medicinals. Pound together
equal quantities of shallots and garlic, mix
these, it says, with wine and the gall of a bull
and leek. Let these mingle together nine days
in a brass vessel, the kind purchased from a
Home Depot. Bathe the afflicted parts in the
froth, as the organism can settle spaciously,
in the sites of endocarditis or infections of
the bones and joints, mastitis, attaching to
the surface of metallic prosthetics, abscesses
of the spleen, the kidney, the spine, necrotizing
fasciitis. The wind of the blood gusts against
her membranes. Apply the formula in a timely
fashion, clown, quickly now.

Breathing Turquoise

During the fat years of Cripple Creek, the
veins of turquoise lay at angles to the seams
of sylvanite and gold, and they say that
when the ore was crushed and cyanidated,
turquoise and the other worthless rocks
were ground into tailings in the stamp
mills, later used as gravel to pave the muddy
streets. Today, small and jagged pieces of
blue after hard rains still surface in the
alleys, washed and alloyed, stonefruit.

That wet morning behind the Elks, by the
pallets and the bone weeds, I found it
and rolled it between my thumb and finger
as I would hold a nipple, a small ball, a
caterpillar, and I placed it in my mouth, to
taste it for breath, for solidity, to conjure
the undisturbed earth, and it worked—my
senses stream like neutrinos through the
core, the clear puddle where I stood, a
philter, a caldera.

Inhabited Letters

We've used up all the names: progress, revolt, revolution, terrorism, wars of national liberation, genocide. We have exhausted our language trying to paper over with words what we know will come.
—Charles Bowden

The word comes about from Latin, *libri*
manu scripti, for the origin of books, the
sheets of parchment, lapped and corrugated,
gathered up together, fastened at the fold,
written by hand, a place we live within.

The furrow of continents, of plates of
floating rock, speak in the coast here,
smeared up with its thin vertical lines
of ocotillo, of wind stunted *opuntia* the
Pinacate, its lower, broken slopes less
fall than migrate to the water, salt marshes,
open horizon, the end, the Sea of Cortez,
searching, I imagine, at any rate not yet
there.

So in the center of the book is the deep
furrow, the place of clasping and disruption,
where the things we care to keep apart lie
stratified or when the book is opened,
posed together.

When I was a child we came here, fished
in blue and red boats deep in the morning
fog, coasting the guano caked sea rocks
for *totuava*, throwing the guts ripped out
through the mouth into the water, flushed
in with us, later floating shallow with the
down tides on the rippled sand.

The ink the book makers took from iron
gall and lampblack, the colors from egg
white drawn into pigments, from plants,
from soil. They burnished the gold powder
into the opposing pages, illumination, we
call it, as if all elements could glow.

And I don't know, I distrust, what is like
what, or how we live within the language
anymore, or how we resort like this to its
analogs, its overlaps. On the sea coast
here the only books are *retablos*, painted
on alters, high and wooden, fancied up for
saints' days and defense.

In the enlarged first letter of the text, the
creatures lived and died. The way the
scribe's typography marked the beginning
of a chapter maybe, some division, the
small worlds of mortality within, bodies
entwined upon the strokes, the serifs,
down, ascending, the characters, like
we are double, and signs of words we
speak and living things could be the same,
a project of keyboards, a pornography.

When the fiberglass boats return to the
shore, the fishermen drop their three
anchors, the two pushed off in shallow
water, the one a nylon rope, pulled up
the dry sand, wrapped around the rebar
rusted into the orange concrete. These
are pages plaited back again.

The early book makers created many
kinds of books, antiphonals, breviaries,
divine offices, missals, the psalter. One,
the book of hours, they used for private
devotion, calendars, psalms, prayers,
passages, and hymns, language done best
and necessarily alone. These no longer exist.

Knife Knife

This has proven an ineffective
tool for killing a small snake.
The animal's immaculate and
transparent teeth leave elliptical
bites over my skin and fluid on
my shirtsleeve. This has become
messy, embarrassing. I look
around the yard to see if anyone
has noticed my botched crime,
this hideous attempt. But in the
end, of course, I am alone. At
least when I write I have the use
of my other hand. I hold the
paper firmly to the counter and
it becomes simply a matter of
forming the letters over and over,
hoping that when it all dries,
enough minerals or other trace
impurities in the water, the
orpiment, cinnabar, the carnalite,
will remain from the knife's
short lines and curves to be read.

Love Charm

A traditional Cherokee formula, freely adapted from a translation by James Mooney (I have changed and moved around certain things, to make sure that it is not accidently sacred); Mooney entitles his translation of the formula "Concerning Living Humanity—Love Charm."

Here you are at rest, a woman white from the dawn,
     and no one is ever lonely when with you.

You are beautiful, and instantly you have created this,
     and now no one is ever lonely when with me.

Here you have placed me,
     so I stand upon the earth.

You have put me here,
     and I shall be in it as it moves about.

This woman's soul has come to rest at the edge of
     her body.

Notes:
—In Cherokee, white (*u-ne:-g*) is associated with happiness; other colors are less satisfactory.
—Beautiful (*u-wo'-du*) means physical beauty and also wholeness; when used to describe a woman it sometimes suggests power, in some cases in decision-making and war.
—To be lonely is worse than it is in English—it not only means being lonesome and alone, but also suggests a kind of degradation.

Tamarix pentandra

*They are weedy, grasping trees that form ugly thickets and are fire hazards,
an introduced pest that adds nothing to the beauty of the river.*
        —Ann Zwinger

Along the length of Labyrinth Canyon, deep thickets
of salt cedar, they call it, *tamarisco*, tamarisk, *pino
salado*, crowd the wide bottomlands of the river in
unbroken walls of green.

The question of what should remain pertains here,

from Red wash, Bull Bottom, past the Trin-Alcove,
the length of Tenmile, the wrap around the great
Bowknot bend, Tidwell, Horsethief Bottom, Woodruff,
Horseshoe Canyon, its meander, and as far as the lake,
the Gila, and on south.

The tamarisk stirs in the up canyon wind, floats dense
mats of roots into the green water, the new cutbanks,
free like the loose hair of men, women, an iodine dye
to the invisible current.

Past miles of it we drifted, looking by mid-afternoon
for open space to camp. Its carmine racemes, stalked
and trailing in the mobile air, the newest flowers
flushed to the end, opened by the feet of bees, the
swarms of flies within its branches, scaled needles,
blue and wet. Its flowers tassel at the ends, where on
rocks the herons stalk and fly ahead.

This machine they believe will kill the tamarisk, or
this other. They bulldoze it where there are roads,
cut it, burn it, paint its stumps with poison. It is the
mad vegetable violence they do this oriental. But
there is no help, no remedy.

We look for a place to tie off the boat in this forest
of the tamarisk, its smell of wet oil, its air of insects.
We know that things happen to us. We live until
the sweat soaks through, until we fall down, our
clothes saturated and half on.

I pinch a twist of its needles between my teeth and
taste the raging salt from it.

Tearblanket

To alter flesh, use the deciduous catclaw,
the spiculumed acacia, tearblanket its
common name, unpronounceable in
ambiguity. I could describe it to you,
three-thorned, polygamous flowers, pinnate
pods, but you will know it because you will
be bleeding and the alkaloids in the cuts
will be a kind of pleasure, perhaps not
mainstream, but not either unusual.

As for the name itself, because there is no
outside to language, perhaps the thorns once
ripped apart someone's bedding, tangled with
their bodies. Perhaps it lodged, a premise, in
the coarse-woven, sweat-soaked space between
the saddle and the mount. The poultice does
nothing to stop this mad post to modernity.

Or the long *a* could become the long *e* and the
the difference between tare and tier Ricky
Ricardo struggles to understand. The dusted
yellow flowers bloom most heavily in April,
which is the cruelest month, and Jesus wept.
But as much as we hate the fucking plant,
small animals at times seek refuge inside
its lower places from predators. Good for
them, but not everyone escapes.

Think about it as you nail the deer hide to the
splintered battens of the barn. The flattened
black skin, cringing around its still bloody
edges, pulling back from bristling hair, looks
petal-like, fine lobed, and lace. Too dense
for fabric, it curls and cracks. You joke that it
died in a tragic gun cleaning accident. In the
morning you will treat it, with borax, salt,
vinegar, with brains. Say the word—tearblanket.
And you have already committed. A living
animal has no edges, you know.

Urine for the Spring

We have no need for a pot of urine. Ours
        has sat unused in the corner for a
        month as it is.

The weather has been clear and cold at
        night. The horizons have been
        far away and have spoken to us
        in the darkness of what we fear
        in what we know of the next town.

There the people all wear coyote masks
        and eat raw meat from chickens.

Urine sits still and thick. This grows
        demeaning for us, in the warmth
        of the wood stove.

We would walk to the next town if the
        roads were open, but they are dark
        and still and empty as snow lies
        three feet deep on the grade.

There are stories about the way they
        copulate in the next town.

And the moon is new and like a branch
        bowed under the snow. We have
        urine stored up from all of us for
        spring.

Metropolis.

To Treat the Black Yellowness

Turtle Island—the old/new name for the continent, based on many creation myths of the people who have been living here for millennia, and reapplied by some of them to "North America" in recent years.
—Gary Snyder

Guiding the rental car north on the Interstate out
of Phoenix, I understand again that in the reciprocal
experience of disease, the complexity of intrusion
shapes the cure.

Driving to find the edge of the glistening buildings,
to get north, to New River and Rock Springs and
into Black Canyon, to traverse into the mountains
from the blue-hot pavement, I seek the intruder, to
suck it out of the body of this place, to send it,
somehow, back.

U tal-e'gwahi didulta'histi ulsge'ta.
Usinu'li datitu'lene'i.

In the great lake beneath the desert, the intruder
occupies itself, pumping from a thousand wells
the fossil water beneath Salt River, Gila River,
the hidden aquatic spaces of the temporary desert.

But in the true diseases that afflict us, there are
no lessons of history. Naming the disease does not
make it universal, as if another can have it too.
Everything must happen for the first time.

The patient is tired, has bad dreams, looks black
around the eyes, falls down.

When they dream of snakes.
When they dream of fish.
When ghosts trouble them.
When the food is changed.

And with the Black Yellowness, the abdomen
swells first, the tips of the fingers turn dark,
and finally, at the end, the throat closes.

And as the sun sets, I push the car quickly up
the last grades, along the Agua Fria to the northwest,
to Yavapai. And of course, the healers had seen
enough to suspect the turtle and to know that
revengeful animals like the turtle and the terrapin
were behind it all, so with an infusion of juniper bark,
you rub the breast and abdomen, while you sing.

Go ahead, sing it.

Protecting Against Overwork

A labour standards office in Tokyo later attributed her death to karoshi
(death from overwork).
        —*The Guardian*

You monitor the reflective margin where the sun
mimics the final energy of the waves as they recede
from the sand. You try to move laterally with it,
flank it, avoid it. Finally you turn and walk directly
into the surf, Kate Chopin submerging in what you
have already embraced. These are the dangers.

Your pulse beats too quickly, captive, faintly. It
does not stop. If you masturbated, that might
calm you. You are awake at 3am, alone. You lie
on the office floor, and your mind catalogs, your
blood does not fill your organs. Your climax fails,
and you give it up. There may be no cure.

Beneath the surface of the ocean the sunken camps
of the hunters layer in sediment. Their route skirted
the shore south from Beringia as the glaciers ebbed
inland. You seek here their warm-drowned hearths.

You are unable to think of your family, of climate
change, of the summer, of gun violence, of your ex-
lover, of god. So think of what is undone, what
remains, what will happen tomorrow and how you
will push and piss out your final liquids, suddenly
so there, sap still soft, prescient bead of amber.

There must be someone to call. They find in the
submerged camps tools, charcoal, the remains of
butchered animals. These are images to focus on
as you say the charms that might protect you.
Stone object. Wooden anthropomorth. Words red
as odem disks drilled to string. Place these within
your clothing. Then never leave the office after.

The Red Deer Site

We remember temporary places, how we wake
there and move
on. The uneven vertical surfaces of the mesa, the
rim rock and

human midden, here the idiom of glyphs soften
place with
the deep instability of time. And we drink cold water
from the plastic cans,

linger in our camp on the edge where beneath that
rough cusp, red deer
browse the south facets of basalt, precisely excised
with stone tools, daubed

red with iron and clay eight hundred years before, the
old people sharpening
their tools of chert, mixing deep pigment to mark
this line between

moments and durations, the vertical limit of the desert,
the beginning of
nothing. Here someone maybe thought to code
impermanence,

to guard against a ghost of distance, and nest bright
deer as their warning.
The people who lived here are today called the
Mountain Hohokam,

a word from the O'odham language, all used up, they
say it means in
English. We have no idea why red deer might inhabit
these things.

Regarding Insect Collapse

The last known Xerces blue was netted by Berkeley alumnus and later UC Davis entomologist W. Harry Lange '33, in the Presidio on March 23, 1941. "I always thought there would be more," he lamented later. "I was wrong."
        —Pat Joseph

The sheer, travertine wings of the Xerces were
combed gently in brown to their edges. The
narratives of Herodotus in the *Histories* tell

of the insect. The wafting pheromones of its
larvae, they say, prompted a social response
from certain species of ants, who took the

Xerces into their colonies to feed them, care
for them. But that was not enough. The
Xerces pioneered our processes. Ordovician–

Silurian, Late Devonian, Permian, Triassic,
Cretaceous, Anthropocene, and *dermestidae*,
the skin beetles, eating also hair, hide, feathers,

fur, everything but bone. These are but two
of them all, the uncounted, one immobile in
its wax museum, one the predator of the proteins

of the dead. The terylene tent of the Malaise
trap flutters like phantom wings in the air
empty of bodies. To preserve an insect, capture

it in the glass cylinder of the trap where ethanol
will work quickly as the killing agent, an act
of pure nostalgia. When the animal is dead,

transport it to the collection. Place it carefully
on the block, holding it with forceps. They are

pinned through the thorax. Leave 3/8 inch of the
pin showing above the body, then pose appendages

and wing-spread accordingly. Display this in a
wooden case under shining glass, as within a
slide. Repeat this several million times until

you have a vast library. This is serious, a race
between the *dermestidae* and us. Hurry.

Raven Mocker

From the size of the holes you can guess at the size of the bullets.
        —Barry Lopez

As it drops low above the houses, the raven
mocker listens for the children through the
black tarred roofs, the windows open to the
evening's first cool air. Small shreds of blue
lead paint lie like the discarded shells of seeds
in the gravel of the yard.

The cannibal ghost, or witch some people call
it, *Kal'lanu Ahyeli'ski* in the language itself,
because with its arms spread out it resembles
the form of the raven. And this is the fear that
slowly wears me down, the fear of a thing I
do not believe.

When a raven dives, it folds one wing close
to its body and falls, turning over in the air as
it drops to earth, crying in a way it never
otherwise does. This sound the raven mocker
apes. *Ysi-ge'yu,* it says, which means beloved,

and *Tsi-hye?-a,* I am devouring my prey, the
recently killed, live things. These are sounds
said to please small children.

And I start to make a list of the things:

There are homes where you can feel its presence.
There are public places.
It is a man and it is a woman.
It is the disappearance of love.
It lives in the danger for children—

They could disappear, be in the darkness beneath the bridge, never wake, never see, drown while bathing, they steal pints of vodka. They are sick and vomiting, and we are all in trouble, and he is hitting the child in anger, and they have no homes. They fight hard with their small hands to pull the bottle of pills from their mother's mouth, and they fall while dancing. They are cut. They cannot be hidden in the dumpster. They make no sound as if it were already over. And this is what always happens with my list.

The hard excrescence of the raven's beak is
horn-like. It grows slowly. It curves slightly,
the same material as the fingernails of a man
or a woman, grown from inside through the
soft skin out. From the sill of the open window,
the raven mocker steps inside, invisible and
during sleep, to take the lap of blood it throws
back into its insatiable throat.

So some trust that the absence of blood around
the mouth of a bird is a sign that all is well, and
there are those who say the brilliant line of a
meteor rids the night of darker things that fall
one-winged to earth, and many of the old ones
simply forbid us to speak of these things at all.

But I say if the children tell you about some
movement in the dark, listen to them.

Desert Center

It takes three years, the therapist said, and
I wanted to stay there for a while, hearing
that over again, maybe passing a cigarette
back and forth a few feet from the words
like they were air rippled from the fumes of
gasoline.

On the way between Kingman
and LA, the town scatters its debris for a
mile beside the interstate, the hollow engine
compartments of trucks, stucco motels boarded
ineffectively against squatters, date palms
collapsing into themselves during their slow
dying, sterile lengths of rusted well casing
stacked on pallets, never to push into the pith
of earth. The center of the desert has not
been calculated. It is not mapped.

An arid wind rakes the surface taking away
the smaller particles. The temperature becomes
spatial. The granite that remains holds heat
poorly, and the emptiness is a conduit to space.
It takes three years, she said, and then you're
better.

Enhance Sexual Performance (male version)

So Dana sits and Hamletizes by the Pacific.
    —D.H. Lawrence

First purchase online supplements—
red ginseng, gingko biloba, maca,
black peppercorn, horny goat weed,
dong quai, yohimbe, L-Arginine.

Sgë!

Brown has no mythological significance,
but find a brown stone, a well-shaped,
rounded, water-worn rock, reddish,
with inclusions of quartz, if possible.

Suspend this from a string. It should
swing in the desired direction or the
contrary one. You may correct for that.

Several of these stones have been obtained
and are now deposited in the Smithsonian.

Preventing the Death of a Loved One

In *Opuntia fulgida*, the axillary buds of the leaves can themselves produce flowers so there are flowers borne on flowers. *Opuntia fulgida* can repeat this...so many times that as the flowers each mature into fruits, there are fruits hanging from fruits hanging from fruit...the common name is "chain fruit cholla."
        —James Mauseth

This is not possible.
        Falling in a shallow plume,
        the thin dermis of the primordia
Orange to brown to red,
        downwind across the sand alluvial
        of a wash, decorticated,
Colors of the paper once folded tight around
        a space of air, a globe, the
        lantern resists.
The fruit remains attached.

Transport by Dry Ravel

Dry ravel is a general term that describes the rolling, bouncing, and sliding of individual particles down a slope and is a dominant hillslope sediment transport process in steep arid and semiarid landscapes.
        —*Emmanuel J. Gabet*

Transport by dry ravel the high places above
the metropolitan valley in a way that is as
automatic as an automaton, but a machine of
place displacing. And this one is done for me,
a prayer flag blowing on the mountain, *Lung ta*,
the Wind Horse. There is no need for a formula.
The southern escarpment of the San Gabriel
range mobilizes incrementally and collapses
with infinite slowness to the plane. My home
is a precarious place built of wood and glass
and language, exposed to the dry aeolian processes,
the frightening things here lead me back to
what is known, what is familiar, and the small
flumes of dry ravel form on the exposed slopes
behind me, countless minute rivulets of sediment,
stopping by night, resuming by day in the dryness,
as if wanting to be seen, not seeking any false
privacy of home. When the air stills, I can hear
the movements, the micro collisions of gravity
across the contour width of slope, sometimes
accumulating on small shelves, then sliding off—
spaying, doubling, involuntary repetition, violating
incrementally the angle of repose. So I sit here
on the mountain like the sorehead loner from
Walden Pond—economy, reading, sounds, solitude,
and Los Angeles is the hungry wormlion toward
which I plummet slothfully in this house of mind.
It is easy. I don't have to do a damn thing to make
this happen.

You Can Eliminate Orange Traffic Cones

You have done the rest. Good job,
and only this remains.

Remember the woman at the coffee
house, back by the sofa with the
chess board, the one who told you
when to travel and when to stay,
and how small seeds should be
swallowed with which liquids,
especially the black sesame, and
how to carve away soft material that
does not belong around the image.

She was an actuary, in her early forties,
and she smelled of grapefruit, and she
told you which non-native plants must
not be used, and of course why the
white rook was missing from the set

She brought it up, but in the end taught
you nothing useful about the cones,
the brightly colored thermoplastic thugs.

You must handle it yourself now.
Create an aqueous infusion of polyps,
extract alkaloids, maintain the regime
of kombucha, sulphuric ether that
will protect against unwanted oriental-
isms and depositions. You know the
rule of cones.

Soon strangers will begin staring at you
with looks of great concern and for some,
anger, but you know how to handle that.
Now you can move at liberty. You are
free.

Reuben Ellis is Professor and Interim Dean of the College of Liberal Arts at Woodbury University in Los Angeles. His Ph.D. is in literature studies from the University of Colorado at Boulder. At Woodbury, he teaches courses in the Professional Writing degree, the first year composition program, and the College of Liberal Art's Interdisciplinary Studies program. His teaching interests include creative writing, periodical writing, newspaper journalism, travel writing, sustainability studies, fiction, and literature. His publications include *Vertical Margins: Mountaineering and the Landscapes of Neo-Imperialism; Stories and Stone: Writing the Ancestral Pueblo Homeland;* and *Beyond Borders: The Selected Essays of Mary Austin*, as well as many published essays, short stories, and poems. His work has appeared in *Journal of Ecocriticism, Western American Literature, MAWA, The Journal of American Culture, South Dakota Review, North Dakota Quarterly, Journal of American Studies, Extrapolation, Papers on Language and Literature, Colby Library Quarterly, Southwestern American Literature, Scroll in Space, En Passant Poetry Quarterly, Wind Literary Journal, New Infinity Review, Aag Aag*, and others. His current book project, *The Last Place on Earth* looks at contemporary experience in the American southwest through the lens of ancient Puebloan ruins and rock art. He enjoys spending time in the wild and open spaces of the American southwest. When he doesn't have a book or a keyboard in front of him, he can be found—or not found—somewhere past the last road. Ellis writes, "a formula can be a performative utterance that enacts, commands, or expresses desire. It is involved with action, change, declaration. A formula can be true or false, happy or unhappy, or it can perhaps fit words to the world. The widely held existence of formulas across cultures and times suggests that the world is dangerous, unstable, a place and experience we seek to control, mitigate, reverse. Believed in, formulas testify to our assertion of potency and influence, both the receptivity and compellability of the external and the constraints of what can be done, but also said."